The Everyday Soup Cookb[o]
Soup Recipes Inspired by th[e] ...ean Diet

by **Alissa Noel Grey**
Text copyright(c)2016 Alissa Noel Grey

Tony,

I hope you find some good soups in here !!

Merry Christmas 2018

Love,
Tessa

Table Of Contents

Healthy Mediterranean Soups for Dinner Tonight

We just love the cozy feeling of sitting down with our family to a home-cooked dinner! But we also live in an age when we are constantly on the move and putting a home-cooked meal on the table during a busy weeknight looks like an impossible endeavor. In my new cookbook I have gathered the very best of my family recipes for homemade soups, inspired by my Mediterranean origins, and prepared using simple and easy to find ingredients. All my recipes have a few things in common – they are healthy, they are family-friendly, and they can be prepared even by an inexperienced cook.

Cooking at home allows you to control the ingredients in your food, so you can use natural ingredients instead of unhealthy processed foods. It also helps control the amount of salt and oils you use in your recipes. Cooking at home provides a way to create delicious soups with a good balance of protein, carbohydrates and fat, plus all the vitamins and minerals you and your loved ones need.

Preparing soups at home may seem hard at the beginning but it soon turns out to be an amazingly rewarding experience. While store bought soups are usually prepared with low-grade ingredients and are sky-high in sodium, homemade soups are filling, flavor-packed and make the perfect healthy meal.

The recipes in this book are inspired by my Mediterranean family recipes and are excellent options to whip up on a weeknight. They do not require complicated cooking techniques and are simply the best solution for fast-paced families who want tasty and healthy meals. Oh, and they taste delicious, too!

For me, preparing healthy family soups is just another way to give and share love. My Mediterranean soup recipes will satisfy even the pickiest eaters while pleasing the whole family!

How to Follow the Mediterranean Diet

The Mediterranean diet is not actually a "diet." Yes, it will help you lose weight and improve your health but it is really more of a relaxed and family-oriented lifestyle. It is living, cooking and eating with enthusiasm and love. People who live in the Mediterranean countries like Greece, Spain, France, Italy, Turkey and Morocco eat mainly local, everyday products that can be bought around the corner or grown in their own backyard. The Mediterranean way of cooking is in reality healthy home cooking embracing a variety of fresh ingredients such as whole grains, healthy fats, more colorful vegetables and fish, and less meat, and using wine, olive oil and fragrant herbs to create rich flavors.

Mediterranean salads are delicious, as well as diet-friendly, because they are usually served with low-carb dressings made with good fats, such as the mono-unsaturated fats found in olive oil, avocados and nuts, and lemon juice, fresh herbs and spices. Mediterranean soups and cooked meals are generally prepared slowly, all in one pot , starting with aromatic vegetables such as garlic, onions, carrots and celery gently sautéed in olive oil. Vegetable broth or water is then added, followed by herbs and spices, your choice of protein sources like fish, chicken or beans, then more vegetables, and perhaps some pasta. The ingredients which need the shortest cooking time are added last.

Unlike many diets that involve increasing your intake of certain vitamins and minerals, with the Mediterranean diet you can always improvise, invent, vary recipes, and substitute one ingredient for another. It allows you to eat a wide variety of healthy whole foods in moderation, is high in good fats and dietary fiber and extremely low in saturated fats.

The Mediterranean diet will help you:

- Eat a well-balanced diet of whole natural foods
- Prevent heart disease, diabetes, arthritis, Alzheimer's, Parkinson's and cancer
- Lower cholesterol levels and blood pressure
- Improve cardiovascular health
- Improve brain and eye health
- Eat foods that are high in good fats and dietary fiber
- Lose weight
- Increase energy

Have you ever struggled to lose weight because you couldn't stick to a "diet", or you're tired of lacking energy all the time, or simply want to get rid of all the processed foods in your diet and don't know how to go about it? If that is you - learn about the Mediterranean Diet and make a life changing shift today.

Just remember these rules to be certain that you are really following a Mediterranean diet:

- Eat vegetables with every meal and eat fresh fruit every day;
- Use olive oil when cooking. Use little or no butter at all;
- Include at least two legume meals per week – add lentils, chickpeas or beans to salads, soups or casseroles.
- Include at least two servings of fish per week: oily fish, if possible, such salmon, mackerel, gem-fish, canned sardines and canned salmon;
- Eat smaller portions of lean meat – mainly chicken, lamb, and beef;
- Eat yogurt and cheese in moderation;
- Consume wine in moderation, only with meals;
- Eat nuts, seeds, fresh fruit and dried fruit as snacks and dessert;

Moroccan-style Chicken Soup

Serves: 5-6

Prep time: 30 min

Ingredients:

3-4 skinless, boneless chicken thighs, cut into bite-sized pieces

1 onion, finely cut

2 garlic cloves, chopped

1 small zucchini, peeled and diced

2 cups butternut squash, peeled and cut into bite-sized pieces

2 tbsp tomato paste

4 cups chicken broth

1/3 cup uncooked couscous

1/2 tsp ground cumin

1/4 tsp ground cinnamon

1 tbsp paprika

1 tsp dried basil

2 tsp orange zest

3 tbsp extra virgin olive oil

Directions:

Heat olive oil in a soup pot over medium heat. Gently sauté onion, for 1 minute, stirring. Add in garlic, basil and chicken, and cook for 2-3 minutes, or until chicken is sealed.

Stir in cumin, cinnamon and paprika. Add butternut squash and stir. Dissolve the tomato paste in the chicken broth and add to the soup.

Bring to a boil, reduce heat and simmer for 10-15 minutes.

Stir in couscous, salt, and zucchini and cook until the butternut squash is tender.

Remove from heat, season with salt and pepper to taste, stir in orange rind, and serve.

Mediterranean Chicken Soup

Serves: 6-8

Prep time: 35 min

Ingredients:

3 chicken breast halves

2 carrots, chopped

1 celery stalk, chopped

1/2 onion, chopped

1/3 cup rice

8 cups water

1/2 cup black olives, pitted and halved

salt and black pepper, to taste

1/2 cup fresh coriander, finely cut, to serve

lemon juice, to serve

Directions:

Place chicken breasts in a soup pot together with onion, carrots, celery, salt, black pepper, and water.

Bring to a boil, add in rice and olives, stir, and reduce heat.

Simmer for 30-35 minutes then remove the chicken from the pot and let it cool slightly.

Shred the chicken and return it back to the pot. Stir, and serve sprinkled with fresh coriander and lemon juice.

Greek Chicken Soup

Serves: 4-5

Prep time: 35 min

Ingredients:

3 chicken breast halves, diced

1/3 cup rice

4 cups chicken broth

1 small onion, finely cut

3 raw egg yolks

1/2 cup fresh lemon juice

3 tbsp extra virgin olive oil

1 tsp salt

1/2 tsp black pepper

1/2 cup fresh parsley, finely cut, to serve

Directions:

In a soup pot, heat the olive oil and gently sauté the onion until translucent. Add in the chicken broth and bring to a boil.

Stir in the rice and the chicken, reduce heat, and simmer until the rice is almost done.

Whisk the egg yolks and lemon juice together in a small bowl. Gently add in a cup of the chicken soup whisking constantly. Return this mixture to the chicken soup and stir well to blend. Do not boil any more.

Season with salt and pepper and garnish with finely chopped parsley. Serve hot.

Healthy Chicken and Oat Soup

Serves: 4-5

Prep time: 35 min

Ingredients:

3 chicken breasts, diced

1 small onion, chopped

3 garlic cloves

1/2 cup quick-cooking oats

1 large carrot, chopped

1 red bell pepper, chopped

1 celery rib, chopped

1 tomato, diced

5 cups water

1 bay leaf

1 tsp salt

1/2 cup fresh parsley leaves, finely cut

black pepper, to taste

Directions:

Place the chicken, bay leaf, celery, carrot, onion, red pepper, tomato and salt into a soup pot. Add in water and bring to the boil then reduce heat and simmer for 30 minutes.

Discard the bay leaf, season with salt and pepper, add in the oats and parsley, simmer for 5 more minutes, and serve.

Bean and Chicken Soup

Serves 4-5

Prep time: 40 min

Ingredients:

2-3 bacon strips, chopped

2 cups cooked and diced chicken

1/2 can kidney beans, rinsed and drained

1 small onion, chopped

2 garlic cloves, chopped

3 cups water

1/2 can diced tomatoes, undrained

1 bay leaf

1/2 tsp dried oregano

1/2 tsp dried basil

salt and pepper, to taste

Directions:

In a deep soup pot, gently cook onion and bacon, stirring, for 3-4 minutes. Add in the garlic and cook until just fragrant.

Add in water, tomatoes and seasonings and bring to a boil. Cover, reduce heat and simmer for 30 minutes. Add in chicken and beans. Simmer for five minutes more and serve.

Chicken Vermicelli Soup

Serves 4

Prep time: 40 min

Ingredients:

3 chicken breast halves

1/2 onion, finely cut

1 garlic clove, chopped

1/2 cup vermicelli

1 carrot, grated

4 cups chicken broth

1 tsp salt

1/2 tsp black pepper

1 egg, beaten

2 tbsp lemon juice

Directions:

Place the chicken breasts and the onion in a soup pot together with 4 cups of chicken broth. Add in 1 tsp salt and bring to a boil.

Cook for 30 minutes or until the chicken is cooked through then take it out of the pot, let it cool a little, dice it, and put it back in the soup.

Stir in carrot, garlic and vermicelli. Reduce heat and simmer over medium heat for 5 minutes.

Whisk the egg and lemon juice in a bowl and slowly stir this mixture into the soup. Do not boil it again.

Warm Chicken and Avocado Soup

Serves 4

Prep time: 6-7 min

Ingredients:

2 ripe avocados, peeled and chopped

1 cooked chicken breast, shredded

1 garlic clove, chopped

3 cups chicken broth

salt and black pepper, to taste

fresh coriander leaves, finely cut, to serve

1/2 cup sour cream, to serve

Directions:

Combine avocados, garlic, and chicken broth in a blender. Process until smooth and transfer to a saucepan.

Add in chicken and cook, stirring, over medium heat until the mixture is hot. Serve topped with sour cream and finely cut coriander leaves.

Light Chicken Soup

Serves: 4

Prep time: 35 min

Ingredients:

3 chicken breasts, diced

1 small onion, finely cut

3 garlic cloves

1 potato, peeled and diced

1 large carrot, chopped

1 green pepper, cut

1 small tomato, diced

1 celery rib, chopped

1 bay leaf

5 cups water

1 tsp salt

1/2 cup fresh parsley leaves, finely cut

black pepper, to taste

Directions:

Place the chicken, bay leaf, celery, carrot, onion, pepper, potato, tomato, and salt into a pot with 5 cups of cold water.

Bring to a boil, reduce heat and simmer for 30 minutes. Season with salt and pepper, add in parsley, simmer for 2-3 minutes and serve.

Broccoli and Chicken Soup

Serves: 4

Prep time: 35 min

Ingredients:

4 boneless chicken thighs, diced

1 small carrot, chopped

1 broccoli head, broken into florets

1 garlic clove, chopped

1 small onion, chopped

4 cups water

3 tbsp extra virgin olive oil

1/2 tsp salt

black pepper, to taste

Directions:

In a deep soup pot, heat olive oil and gently sauté broccoli for 2-3 minutes, stirring occasionally. Add in onion, carrot, chicken and cook, stirring, for 2-3 minutes. Stir in salt, black pepper and water. Bring to a boil.

Simmer for 30 minutes then remove from heat and set aside to cool. In a blender or food processor, blend soup until completely smooth.

Asparagus and Chicken Soup

Serves 4

Prep time: 30 min

Ingredients:

2 chicken breast fillets, cooked and diced

2-3 leeks, finely cut

1 bunch asparagus, trimmed and cut

4 cups chicken broth

2 tbsp extra virgin olive oil

1/2 cup fresh parsley, finely chopped

salt and black pepper, to taste

lemon juice, to serve

Directions:

Heat the olive oil in a large soup pot. Add in the leeks and gently sauté, stirring, for 2-3 minutes. Add chicken broth, the diced chicken, and bring to a boil. Reduce heat and simmer for 15 minutes.

Add in asparagus, parsley, salt and black pepper, and cook for 5 minutes more. Serve with lemon juice.

Turkey and Ricotta Meatball Soup

Serves: 4-5

Prep time: 35 min

Ingredients:

1 lb ground turkey meat

1 egg, lightly whisked

1 cup whole milk ricotta

1 cup grated Parmesan cheese

4 tbsp flour

1/2 onion, finely cut

4 cups chicken broth

2 cups baby spinach leaves

1 tsp dried thyme leaves

3 tbsp extra virgin olive oil

½ tsp black pepper

Directions:

Place ground turkey meat, Ricotta, Parmesan, egg and black pepper. Combine well with hands and roll teaspoonfuls of the mixture into balls. Place flour in a shallow bowl and roll each meatball in the flour then set aside on a large plate.

Heat olive oil into a deep soup pot and gently sauté onion until transparent. Add in thyme and broth and bring to a boil.

Stir in meatballs, reduce heat, and simmer, uncovered, for 15 minutes. Add baby spinach and cook for 2-3 more minutes until it wilts.

Spanish Cold Prawn Soup

Serves 8-9

Prep time: 20 min

Ingredients:

3 lbs cooked, peeled and deveined prawn

3 cups tomato juice

3 cups prawn stock

3 spring onions, chopped

3 avocados, peeled and diced

1 cucumber, peeled and diced

2 large tomatoes, diced

1 cup finely chopped parsley

2 tbsp lime juice

salt and pepper, to taste

Directions:

Combine the tomato juice and prawn stock. Stir in the prawns, avocados, cucumber, tomatoes, spring onions, parsley, lime juice, salt and pepper.

Refrigerate until ready to serve.

Mediterranean Fish and Quinoa Soup

Serves: 4-5

Prep time: 30 min

Ingredients:

1 lb cod fillets, cubed

1 onion, chopped

3 tomatoes, chopped

1/2 cup quinoa, rinsed

1 red pepper, chopped

1 carrots, chopped

1/2 cup black olives, pitted and sliced

1 garlic clove, crushed

3 tbsp extra virgin olive oil

a pinch of cayenne pepper

1 bay leaf

1 tsp dried thyme

1 tsp dried dill

½ tsp pepper

½ cup white wine

4 cups water

1/2 cup fresh parsley, finely cut

Directions:

Heat the olive oil over medium heat and sauté the onion, red pepper, garlic and carrot until tender.

Stir in the cayenne pepper, bay leaf, herbs, salt and pepper. Add the white wine, water, quinoa and tomatoes and bring to a boil.

Reduce heat, cover, and cook for 10 minutes. Stir in olives and the fish and cook for another 10 minutes. Stir in parsley and serve hot.

Fish and Noodle Soup

Serves: 6-7

Prep time: 15 min

Ingredients:

4 white fish fillets, cut into strips

2 carrots, cut into ribbons

1 zucchini, peeled and cut into ribbons

5-6 white button mushrooms, sliced

1 celery stalk, finely cut

1 cup baby spinach

7 oz rice noodles

3 cups vegetable broth

2 cups water

3 tbsp soy sauce

1 tsp ground ginger

salt and black pepper, to taste

Directions:

Place vegetable broth, water and soy sauce in a deep soup pot. Bring to a boil and add carrots, celery, zucchini, mushrooms and ginger.

Simmer, partially covered, for 5 minutes then add in the fish and noodles and simmer for 5 minutes more or until the fish is cooked through.

Stir in baby spinach and cook until it wilts. Season with black pepper and salt to taste and serve.

Lamb Soup

Serves 4-5

Prep time: 45-50 min

Ingredients:

2 lbs lean boneless lamb, cubed

1 onion, finely cut

1 carrot, chopped

10-15 spring onions, chopped

4 cups water

2 tbsp extra virgin olive oil

1/2 tsp paprika

black pepper, to taste

1/2 cup fresh mint, finely cut

1/2 cup fresh parsley, finely cut

2 eggs

Directions:

In a deep soup pot, heat olive oil and gently brown the lamb cubes. Add in the onion and carrot and sauté for 2-3 minutes, stirring. Add in paprika and water. Bring to the boil, then lower heat to medium-low and simmer until the lamb softens.

Add spring onions, mint, parsley, salt and black pepper. Bring to a boil again and simmer for 5 minutes.

Whisk the the eggs in a small bowl. Take one ladle from the soup and add into the egg mixture. Stir to combine. Take another ladle and stir again. Pour the egg back into into the soup and stir. Do not boil again. Serve hot.

Hearty Lamb and Vegetable Soup

Serves 4-5

Prep time: 30 min

Ingredients:

2 cups roasted lamb, shredded

4 cups chicken broth

2 tomatoes, diced

1 onion, finely cut

1 carrot, chopped

1 small turnip, chopped

1 celery rib, finely cut

3 tbsp extra virgin olive oil

salt and black pepper, to taste

Directions:

Heat olive oil in a large saucepan and gently sauté onion, carrot, celery and turnip, stirring, for 5 minutes, or until softened.

Add lamb, broth and tomatoes. Bring to the boil then reduce heat and simmer for 20 minutes, or until vegetables are tender.

Season with salt and black pepper to taste.

Libyan Lamb Soup

Serves 4-5

Prep time: 40 min

Ingredients:

1 lb lamb stewing meat

4 cups chicken broth

2 tomatoes, diced

1 onion, finely cut

2 tbsp tomato paste

1 can chickpeas, drained

1 tbsp dried mint

1 tsp ground turmeric

1 tsp ground cinnamon

1 tsp ground coriander

3 tbsp extra virgin olive oil

juice of one lemon

Directions:

Heat olive oil in a large saucepan and gently sauté the onion and lamb meat, stirring, for 5 minutes, or until browned.

Add broth and tomatoes, the tomato paste and spices. Bring to the boil then reduce heat and simmer for 30 minutes, or until lamb is very tender.

Add the chickpeas, the mint, and the lemon juice. Simmer a few minutes more.

Italian Beef and Vegetable Soup

Serves: 4-5

Prep time: 40 min

Ingredients:

2 slices bacon, chopped

1 lb lean ground beef

1 carrot, chopped

2 cloves garlic, finely chopped

1 small onion, chopped

1 celery stalk, chopped

1 bay leaf

1 tsp dried basil

1 cup canned tomatoes, diced and drained

4 cups beef broth

1/2 cup canned chickpeas

½ cup vermicelli

Directions:

In a large soup pot, cook bacon and ground beef until well done, breaking up the beef as it cooks. Drain off the fat and add in onion, garlic, carrot and celery.

Cook for 3-4 minutes until fragrant. Stir in the bay leaf, basil, tomatoes and beef broth. Bring to a boil then reduce heat and simmer for about 20 minutes.

Add the chickpeas and vermicelli. Cook, uncovered, for about 5 minutes more and serve.

Barley Beef Soup

Serves: 4-5

Prep time: 80 min

Ingredients:

12 oz beef stew meat, cut into 1 inch cubes

1 medium leek, chopped

2 garlic cloves, chopped

2 bay leaves

1 can tomatoes (15 oz), diced and drained

1/2 cup barley

1 cup frozen mixed vegetables

4 cups beef broth

3 tbsp extra virgin olive oil

1 tsp paprika

Directions:

Heat oil in a large saucepan over medium-high heat. Sauté beef until well browned. Add in leeks and garlic and sauté until fragrant. Add paprika, beef broth and bay leaves; season with salt and pepper. Cover and bring to a boil then reduce heat and simmer for 60 minutes.

Stir in frozen vegetables, tomatoes, and barley. Return to boiling, reduce heat and simmer, covered, about 15 minutes more or until meat and vegetables are tender. Discard bay leaves and serve.

Hearty Meatball Soup

Serves: 4-5

Prep time: 35 min

Ingredients:

1 lb lean ground beef

1 egg, lightly whisked

1/2 onion, chopped

2 garlic cloves, chopped

1 tomato, diced

2 potatoes, diced

1/2 red bell pepper, chopped

4 cups water

4 tbsp flour

1 cup vermicelli, broken into pieces

½ bunch of parsley, finely cut

3 tbsp extra virgin olive oil

½ tsp black pepper

1 tsp paprika

1 tsp salt

Directions:

Place ground meat, egg, black pepper and salt in a bowl. Combine well with hands and roll teaspoonfuls of the mixture into balls.

Place flour in a shallow bowl and roll each meatball in the flour then set aside on a large plate.

Heat olive oil into a deep soup pot and gently sauté onion and garlic until transparent. Add water and bring to a boil.

Stir in meatballs, carrot, pepper, tomato and potatoes. Reduce heat to low and simmer, uncovered, for 15 minutes.

Add parsley and vermicelli and cook for 5 more minutes. Serve with a dollop of yogurt on top.

Meatball Soup with Spinach

Serves 4-5

Prep time: 30 min

Ingredients:

1 lb ground beef

1 small onion, grated

1 onion, chopped

1 egg, lightly beaten

2 garlic cloves, crushed

1 cup baby spinach, coarsely chopped

4-5 fresh basil leaves, finely chopped

1 cup tomato sauce

3 cups beef broth

2 tbsp extra virgin olive oil

Directions:

Combine ground beef, onion, garlic, and egg in a large bowl. Season with salt and pepper to taste. Mix well with hands and roll teaspoonfuls of the mixture into balls. Place meatballs on a large plate.

Heat olive oil into a large deep saucepan and sauté onion and garlic until transparent. Add in tomato sauce and broth and bring to a boil over high heat. Stir in meatballs.

Reduce heat to medium-low and simmer, uncovered, for 20 minutes. Add in spinach, basil, salt, and pepper and simmer, uncovered, until spinach is wilted, about 1 minute.

Split Pea Soup with Ham and Barley

Serves: 4-5

Prep time: 35 min

Ingredients:

3/4 cup dry yellow split peas

2 carrots, chopped

1/2 lb low-sodium, nitrate-free, lean cooked ham, cut into 1/2-inch cubes

1 zucchini, peeled and diced

1 potato, peeled and diced

1 cup quick-cooking pearl barley

2 tsp dried sage

4 cups water

4 tbsp extra virgin olive oil

salt and black pepper, to taste

Directions:

In a medium pot, bring 2 cups water to a boil on high heat. Add split peas and reduce heat to medium-low. Simmer, uncovered, for 20 minutes. Drain and set aside.

Gently heat olive oil in a large soup pot. Add in onions, carrot and ham and cook for 1-2 minutes, stirring, until vegetables are tender.

Add in zucchini, sage, barley and water. Season to taste with salt and pepper and simmer for 15 minutes.

Mushroom and Kale Soup

Serves: 4-5

Prep time: 30 min

Ingredients:

1 onion, chopped

1 carrot, chopped

1 zucchini, peeled and diced

1 potato, peeled and diced

10 white mushrooms, chopped

1 bunch kale (10 oz), stemmed and coarsely chopped

3 cups vegetable broth

4 tbsp extra virgin olive oil

salt and black pepper. to taste

Directions:

Gently heat olive oil in a large soup pot. Add in onions, carrot and mushrooms and cook until vegetables are tender.

Stir in the zucchini, kale and vegetable broth. Season to taste with salt and pepper and simmer for 20 minutes.

Creamy Brussels Sprout Soup

Serves: 4-5

Prep time: 30 min

Ingredients:

1 lb frozen Brussels sprouts, thawed

2 potatoes, peeled and chopped

1 large onion, chopped

3 garlic cloves, minced

4 cups vegetable broth

3 tbsp extra virgin olive oil

1/2 tsp curry powder

salt and black pepper, to taste

Directions:

Gently heat olive oil in a large saucepan over medium-high heat. Cook onion and garlic and for 3-4 minutes until tender. Add in Brussels sprouts, potato, curry and vegetable broth.

Cover and bring to a boil, then reduce heat and simmer for 20 minutes, stirring from time to time.

Remove from heat and blend until smooth. Return to pan and cook until heated through.

Creamy Potato Soup

Serves: 4-5

Prep time: 35 min

Ingredients:

6 medium potatoes, cut into small cubes

1 leek, white part only, chopped

1 carrot, chopped

1 zucchini, peeled and chopped

1 celery stalk, chopped

3 cups water

1 cup milk

3 tbsp extra virgin olive oil

salt and black pepper, to taste

Directions:

Gently heat olive oil in a deep saucepan and sauté the onion for 2-3 minutes. Add in potatoes, carrot, zucchini and celery and cook for 2-3 minutes, stirring.

Add in water and salt and bring to a boil, then lower heat and simmer until the vegetables are tender. Blend until smooth, add milk, blend some more and serve.

Leek, Brown Rice and Potato Soup

Serves: 4-5

Prep time: 35 min

Ingredients:

3 potatoes, peeled and diced

2 leeks, finely chopped

1/4 cup brown rice

5 cups water

3 tbsp extra virgin olive oil

lemon juice, to taste

Directions:

Heat olive oil in a deep soup pot and sauté leeks for 3-4 minutes. Add in potatoes and cook for a minute more.

Stir in water, bring to a boil, and the brown rice. Reduce heat and simmer for 30 minutes. Add lemon juice, to taste, and serve.

Fast Mediterranean Chickpea Soup

Serves: 5-6

Prep time: 30 min

Ingredients:

1 can (15 oz) chickpeas, drained

1 small onion, chopped

2 garlic cloves, minced

1 can (15 oz) tomatoes, diced

2 cups vegetable broth

1 cup milk

3 tbsp extra virgin olive oil

2 bay leaves

1/2 tsp dried oregano

Directions:

Heat olive oil in a deep soup pot and sauté onion and garlic for 1-2 minutes. Add in broth, chickpeas, tomatoes, bay leaves, and oregano.

Bring the soup to a boil then reduce heat and simmer for 20 minutes. Add in milk and cook for 1-2 minutes more. Set aside to cool, discard the bay leaves and blend until smooth.

Tunisian Chickpea Soup

Serves:

Prep time: 30 min

Ingredients:

1 can (15 oz) chickpeas, drained

1 small onion, chopped

2 garlic cloves, minced

4 cups vegetable broth

2 tbsp Harissa Paste

3 tbsp extra virgin olive oil

2 tsp cumin

juice of one lemon

fresh parsley, finely cut, to serve

yogurt, to serve

poached eggs, to serve

Directions:

Heat olive oil in a deep soup pot and sauté onion and garlic for 1-2 minutes. Add in broth, chickpeas, lemon juice and cumin.

Bring the soup to a boil then reduce heat and simmer for 30 minutes. Serve with fresh parsley, yogurt or poached eggs.

Creamy Tomato and Roasted Pepper Soup

Serves: 4-5

Prep time: 35 min

Ingredients:

1 (12-ounce) jar roasted red peppers, drained and chopped

1 large onion, chopped

2 garlic cloves, minced

4 medium tomatoes, chopped

4 cups vegetable broth

3 tbsp extra virgin olive oil

2 bay leaves

Directions:

Heat olive oil in a large saucepan over medium-high heat and sauté onion for 3-4 minutes, stirring. Add in garlic and sauté until just fragrant.

Stir in the red peppers, bay leaves and tomatoes and simmer for 10 minutes. Add broth, season with salt and pepper, and bring to the boil.

Reduce heat and simmer for 20 minutes. Set aside to cool slightly, remove the bay leaves and blend, in batches, until smooth.

Fast Red Lentil Soup

Serves: 4-5

Prep time: 20 min

Ingredients:

1 cup red lentils

1/2 small onion, chopped

2 garlic cloves, chopped

1/2 red pepper, chopped

3 cups vegetable broth

1 cup coconut milk

3 tbsp extra virgin olive oil

1 tbsp paprika

1/2 tsp ginger

1 tsp cumin

salt and black pepper, to taste

Directions:

Gently heat olive oil in a large saucepan. Add onion, garlic, red pepper, paprika, ginger and cumin and sauté, stirring, until just fragrant. Add in red lentils and vegetable broth.

Bring to a boil, cover, and simmer for 20 minutes. Add in coconut milk and simmer for 5 more minutes.

Remove from heat, season with salt and black pepper, and blend until smooth. Serve hot.

Mediterranean Lentil Soup

Serves: 4-5

Prep time: 35 min

Ingredients:

1 cup red lentils

2 carrots, chopped

1 onion, chopped

1 garlic clove, chopped

1 small red pepper, chopped

1 can tomatoes, chopped

½ can chickpeas, drained

½ can white beans, drained

1 small celery stalk, chopped

6 cups water

1 tbsp paprika

1 tsp ginger, grated

1 tsp cumin

3 tbsp extra virgin olive oil

Directions:

Heat olive oil in a deep soup pot and gently sauté onions, garlic, red pepper and ginger. Add in water, lentils, chickpeas, white beans, tomatoes, carrots, celery, and cumin.

Bring to a boil then lower heat and simmer for 35 minutes, or until the lentils are tender. Purée half the soup in a food processor. Return the puréed soup to the pot, stir and serve.

Pea and Dill Soup with Rice

Serves: 4

Prep time: 25 min

Ingredients:

1 (16 oz) bag frozen green peas

1 onion, chopped

3-4 garlic cloves, chopped

1/3 cup rice

3 tbsp fresh dill, chopped

3 tbsp extra virgin olive oil

fresh dill, finely chopped, to serve

salt and pepper, to taste

Directions:

Heat oil in a large saucepan over medium-high heat and sauté onion and garlic for 3-4 minutes.

Add in peas and vegetable broth and bring to the boil. Stir in rice, cover, reduce heat, and simmer for 15 minutes. Add dill, season with salt and pepper and serve sprinkled with fresh dill.

Minted Pea and Nettle Soup

Serves: 4

Prep time: 25 min

Ingredients:

1 onion, chopped

3-4 garlic cloves, chopped

4 cups vegetable broth

2 tbsp dried mint leaves

1 16 oz bag frozen green peas

about 20 nettle tops

3 tbsp extra virgin olive oil

fresh dill, finely chopped, to serve

Directions:

Heat oil in a large saucepan over medium-high heat and sauté onion and garlic for 3-4 minutes.

Add in dried mint, peas, washed nettles, and vegetable broth and bring to the boil. Cover, reduce heat, and simmer for 10 minutes. Remove from heat and set aside to cool slightly, then blend in batches, until smooth. Return soup to saucepan over medium-low heat and cook until heated through. Season with salt and pepper. Serve sprinkled with fresh dill.

Bean and Pasta Soup

Serves: 4-5

Prep time: 10-15 min

Ingredients:

1 onion, chopped

2 large carrots, chopped

2 garlic cloves, minced

1 cup cooked orzo

1 15 oz can white beans, rinsed and drained

1 15 oz can tomatoes, diced and undrained

1 cup baby spinach leaves

3 cups vegetable broth

1 tbsp paprika

1 tbsp dried mint

3 tbsp extra virgin olive oil

salt and black pepper, to taste

Directions:

Heat the olive oil over medium heat and gently sauté the onion, garlic and carrots. Add in tomatoes, broth, salt and pepper, and bring to a boil.

Reduce heat and cook for 5-10 minutes, or until the carrots are tender. Stir in orzo, beans and spinach, and simmer until spinach is wilted.

Tuscan Bean Soup

Serves: 4-5

Prep time: 10-15 min

Ingredients:

1 onion, chopped

1 large carrot, chopped

2 garlic cloves, minced

1 15 oz can white beans, rinsed and drained

1 cup spinach leaves, trimmed and washed

3 cups vegetable broth

1 tbsp paprika

1 tbsp dried mint

3 tbsp extra virgin olive oil

salt and black pepper, to taste

Directions:

Heat the olive oil over medium heat and gently sauté the onion, garlic and carrot. Add in beans, broth, salt and pepper and bring to a boil.

Reduce heat and cook for 10 minutes, or until the carrots are tender. Stir in spinach, and simmer for about 5 minutes, until spinach is wilted.

Italian Vegetable Soup

Serves: 4-5

Prep time: 25 min

Ingredients:

1/2 onion, chopped

2 garlic cloves, chopped

¼ cabbage, chopped

1 carrot, chopped

2 celery stalks, chopped

3 cups water

1 cup canned tomatoes, diced, undrained

1 1/2 cup green beans, trimmed and cut into 1/2-inch pieces

1/2 cup pasta, cooked

2-3 fresh basil leaves

2 tbsp extra virgin olive oil

black pepper and salt, to taste

Directions:

Heat the olive oil in a large pot over medium-high heat. Add the onion and cook until translucent, about 4 minutes. Add in the garlic, carrot and celery and cook for 5 minutes more.

Stir in the green beans, cabbage, tomatoes, basil, and water and bring to a boil.

Reduce heat and simmer uncovered, for 15 minutes, or until vegetables are tender. Stir in pasta, season with pepper and salt to taste and serve.

French-style Vegetable Soup

Serves: 4-5

Prep time: 25 min

Ingredients:

2 leeks, white and pale green parts only, well rinsed and thinly sliced

1 large zucchini, peeled and diced

1 medium fennel bulb, trimmed, cored, and cut into large chunks

2 garlic cloves, chopped

3 cups vegetable broth

1 cup canned tomatoes, drained and chopped

1/2 cup vermicelli, broken into small pieces

3 tbsp extra virgin olive oil

black pepper, to taste

Directions:

Heat the olive oil in a large stockpot. Add the leeks and sauté over low heat for 5 minutes. Add in the zucchini, fennel and garlic and cook for about 5 minutes.

Stir in the vegetable broth and the tomatoes and bring to the boil. Reduce heat and simmer, uncovered, for 20 minutes, or until the vegetables are tender but still holding their shape.

Stir in the vermicelli. Simmer for a further 5 minutes and serve.

Ginger-Turmeric Carrot Soup

Serves 5-6

Prep time: 35 min

Ingredients:

2 lb carrots, peeled and chopped

1 medium onion, chopped

4 cups water

3 tbsp extra virgin olive oil

2 cloves garlic, crushed

1 tbsp turmeric

1 tbsp grated fresh ginger

½ bunch, fresh coriander, finely cut

salt and pepper to taste

½ cup heavy cream

Directions:

Heat the olive oil in a large pot over medium heat, and gently sauté the onions, carrots and garlic until tender. Add in salt, pepper, turmeric and ginger and stir. Add water and bring to a boil.

Reduce heat to low and simmer 30 minutes. Transfer the soup to a blender or food processor and blend until smooth. Return to the pot and continue cooking for a few more minutes.

Remove soup from heat and stir in the cream. Serve with coriander sprinkled over each serving.

Spiced Beet and Carrot Soup

Serves: 4-5

Prep time: 25 min

Ingredients:

3 beets, washed and peeled

2 carrots, peeled and chopped

1 small onion, chopped

1 garlic clove, chopped

3 cups vegetable broth

1 cup water

2 tbsp extra virgin olive oil

1 tsp grated ginger

1 tsp grated orange peel

Directions:

Heat the olive oil in a large stockpot. Add the onion and sauté over low heat for 3-4 minutes or until translucent. Add the garlic, beets, carrots, ginger and lemon rind. Stir in water and vegetable broth and bring to the boil.

Reduce heat to medium and simmer, partially covered, for 30 minutes, or until beets are tender.

Cool slightly and blend soup in batches until smooth. Season with salt and pepper and serve.

Creamy Cauliflower Soup

Serves: 4-5

Prep time: 35 min

Ingredients:

1 medium head cauliflower, chopped

1 garlic clove, minced

3 cups vegetable broth

1 cup milk

3-4 tbsp extra virgin olive oil

salt, to taste

black pepper, to taste

Directions:

Heat the olive oil in a deep pot over medium heat and gently sauté the cauliflower for 4-5 minutes. Stir in the garlic and vegetable broth and bring to a boil.

Reduce heat, cover, and simmer for 30 minutes. Add in coconut milk and blend in a blender until smooth. Season with salt and pepper to taste and serve.

Pumpkin and Bell Pepper Soup

Serves: 4-5

Prep time: 35 min

Ingredients:

1/2 small onion, chopped

3 cups pumpkin cubes

2 red bell peppers, chopped

1 carrot, chopped

3 cups vegetable broth

3 tbsp extra virgin olive oil

1/2 tsp cumin

salt and black pepper, to taste

Directions:

Heat the olive oil in a deep soup pot and sauté the onion for 4-5 minutes. Add in the pumpkin, carrot and bell peppers and cook, stirring, for 5 minutes.

Stir in broth and cumin and bring to the boil. Reduce heat to low, cover, and simmer, stirring occasionally, for 30 minutes, or until vegetables are soft. Season with salt and pepper, blend in batches and reheat to serve.

Fresh Asparagus Soup

Serves: 4-5

Prep time: 35 min

Ingredients:

2 lb fresh asparagus, cut into 1 inch pieces

1 large onion, chopped

2 garlic cloves, minced

½ cup raw cashews, soaked in warm water for 1 hour

3 cups vegetable broth

3 tbsp extra virgin olive oil

lemon juice, to taste

Directions:

Heat olive oil in a large saucepan over medium-high heat and sauté onion for 3-4 minutes, stirring. Add in garlic and sauté until just fragrant. Stir in asparagus and simmer for 5 minutes.

Add broth, season with salt and pepper and bring to the boil. Reduce heat and simmer for 20 minutes.

Set aside to cool slightly, add cashews, and blend, in batches, until smooth. Season with lemon juice and serve.

Bean and Spinach Soup

Serves: 4-5

Prep time: 10-15 min

Ingredients:

1 onion, chopped

1 large carrot, chopped

2 garlic cloves, minced

1 15 oz can white beans, rinsed and drained

1 cup spinach leaves, trimmed and washed

3 cups vegetable broth

1 tbsp paprika

1 tbsp dried mint

3 tbsp extra virgin olive oil

salt and black pepper, to taste

Directions:

Heat the olive oil over medium heat and gently sauté the onion, garlic and carrot. Add in beans, broth, salt and pepper and bring to a boil.

Reduce heat and cook for 10 minutes, or until the carrots are tender. Stir in spinach, and simmer for about 5 minutes, until spinach is wilted.

Shredded Cabbage Soup

Serves: 4-5

Prep time: 45 min

Ingredients:

1 onion, chopped

1/2 head cabbage, shredded

1 carrot, chopped

1 potato, peeled and diced

1 celery stalk, sliced

1 can (15 oz) diced tomatoes, undrained

3 cups vegetable broth

1 tsp Italian seasoning

3 tbsp extra virgin olive oil

salt and pepper, to taste

Directions:

Heat the oil over medium heat and gently sauté the onion until translucent. Add in cabbage, carrot, potato, celery, tomatoes and seasoning and stir to combine.

Add in the broth, bring the soup to a boil, reduce heat, and simmer for 30-35 minutes. Season with salt and black pepper to taste.

Avocado Gazpacho

Serves 4

Prep time: 5 min

Ingredients:

2 ripe avocados, peeled and chopped

2-3 tomatoes, diced

1 large cucumber, peeled and diced

1/2 small onion, chopped

2 tbsp lemon juice

1 tsp salt

black pepper, to taste

fresh parsley leaves, finely cut, to serve

Directions:

Combine avocados, cucumbers, tomatoes, onion, lemon juice, salt and black pepper in a blender.

Process until smooth and serve sprinkled with chopped parsley leaves.

Spanish Gazpacho Soup

Serves 6

Prep time: 5 min

Ingredients:

9-10 tomatoes, diced

1 onion, chopped

1 green pepper, sliced

1 large cucumber, peeled and sliced

2 garlic cloves

1 tbsp red wine vinegar

salt, to taste

4 tbsp extra virgin olive oil

½ onion, chopped, to serve

1 green pepper, chopped, to serve

1 cucumber, chopped, to serve

Directions:

Place the tomatoes, garlic, onion, green pepper, cucumber, salt, olive oil and vinegar in a blender or food processor and puree until smooth, adding small amounts of cold water if needed.

Refrigerate for 30 minutes and serve with chopped onion, green pepper and cucumber sprinkled over each serving.

Cold Avocado and Cucumber Soup

Serves 4

Prep time: 5 min

Ingredients:

2 ripe avocados, peeled and chopped

3 cucumbers, peeled and chopped

1 green onion, chopped

2 tbsp lime juice

1/2 tsp salt

black pepper, to taste

fresh coriander leaves, finely cut, to serve

Directions:

Combine avocados, cucumbers, onion, lime juice, salt and black pepper in a blender.

Process until smooth and serve sprinkled with chopped coriander leaves.

Yogurt and Cucumber Soup

Serves 4-5

Ingredients:

1 large cucumber, peeled and diced

2 cups Greek yogurt

2 garlic cloves, crushed

2 cups cold water

3 tbsp extra virgin olive oil

1/2 cup fresh dill, very finely cut

1/2 cup crushed walnuts, to serve

Cut the cucumber into very small cubes.

Directions:

In a large glass bowl, dilute the yogurt with water. Add in the cucumber and garlic, stirring to combine.

Season with salt to the taste, stir in dill, and sprinkle with the crushed walnuts. Refrigerate for 10-15 minutes and serve.

Tomato Soup

Serves 4

Prep time: 35 min

Ingredients:

5 cups chopped fresh tomatoes or 1 can diced tomatoes (28 oz), undrained

1 onion, finely cut

1/2 cup vermicelli

2 cups water

1 garlic clove, crushed

3 tbsp extra virgin olive oil

1 tsp salt

½ tsp black pepper

1 tsp sugar

½ cup fresh parsley, finely cut

Directions:

In a soup pot, gently sauté onion and garlic in olive oil. When onion has softened, add in tomatoes and cook, stirring, for 5-6 minutes.

Stir in water, salt, pepper and sugar and cook for 10 minutes then set aside to cool.

Blend with an immersion blender, add in vermicelli, and bring to the boil. Simmer for 10 minutes, stirring occasionally. Sprinkle with parsley and serve.

Carrot, Sweet Potato and Chickpea Soup

Serves: 5-6

Prep time: 35 min

Ingredients:

3 large carrots, chopped

1/2 onion, chopped

1 can (15 oz) chickpeas, undrained

2 sweet potatoes, peeled and diced

4 cups vegetable broth

1/2 cup milk

2 tbsp extra virgin olive oil

1 tsp cumin

1 tsp ginger

salt and pepper, to taste

Directions:

Heat olive oil in a large saucepan over medium heat. Add onion and carrots and sauté until tender. Add in broth, chickpeas, sweet potato and seasonings.

Bring to a boil then reduce heat and simmer, covered, for 30 minutes. Blend soup until smooth, add in milk and cook for 2-3 minutes until heated through.

Creamy Artichoke Soup

Serves: 4-5

Prep time: 20 min

Ingredients:

3 cups artichoke hearts, chopped

1/2 onion, chopped

2 celery stalk, chopped

1 small potato, peeled and chopped

2 garlic cloves, minced

2 cups vegetable broth

1 cup coconut milk

2 tbsp olive oil

1 tsp salt

black pepper, to serve

Directions:

Heat olive oil in a large pot and gently sauté the onion, celery and garlic until just fragrant.

Stir in vegetable broth, coconut milk, artichokes and salt and bring to the boil.

Reduce heat and simmer for 15 minutes. Set aside to cool and blend until smooth. Serve sprinkled with black pepper.

Brown Lentil Soup

Serves: 4-5

Prep time: 35 min

Ingredients:

1 cup brown lentils

1 small onion, chopped

4 garlic cloves, minced

1 medium carrot, chopped

1 medium tomato, diced

3 cups warm water

4 tbsp extra virgin olive oil

1 tbsp paprika

1 tbsp summer savory

Directions:

Heat olive oil in a deep soup pot and cook the onions and carrots until tender. Add in paprika, garlic, lentils, savory and water, stir, and bring to the boil.

Reduce heat and cook, covered, for 30 minutes. Add tomato and salt and simmer for 10 minutes more.

Lemon Artichoke Soup

Serves: 4-5

Prep time: 35 min

Ingredients:

3 cups artichoke hearts, chopped

1/2 onion, chopped

1 celery stalk, chopped

1 carrot, chopped

2 garlic cloves, minced

2 cups vegetable broth

2 tbsp olive oil

1 tsp salt

2 tbsp lemon juice

1 cup coconut milk

Directions:

Heat olive oil in a large pot and gently sauté the onion, celery, carrot, and garlic until the onion and garlic are translucent. Stir in vegetable broth, artichokes and salt and bring to the boil.

Reduce heat, add lemon juice and simmer for 15 minutes. Set aside to cool and blend until smooth.

Stir in coconut milk and simmer for another 5 minutes.

Lentil, Barley and Kale Soup

Serves: 4-5

Prep time: 35 min

Ingredients:

2 medium leeks, chopped

3 garlic cloves, chopped

2 bay leaves

1 can tomatoes (15 oz), diced and undrained

1/2 cup red lentils

1/2 cup barley

1 bunch kale (10 oz), stemmed and coarsely chopped

4 cups water

3 tbsp extra virgin olive oil

1 tsp paprika

½ tsp cumin

Directions:

Heat oil in a large saucepan over medium-high heat. Sauté the leeks and garlic until just fragrant. Add in cumin and paprika, tomatoes, lentils, barley, and water.

Season with salt and pepper. Cover and bring to the boil then reduce heat and simmer for 40 minutes or until the barley is tender.

Add in kale, stir it in, and let it simmer for 3-4 minutes more.

Creamy Parsnip Soup

Serves: 4-5

Prep time: 35 min

Ingredients:

6 slices bacon

5 parsnips, peeled and chopped

1/2 onion, chopped

1 small celery stalk, chopped

1 small potato, peeled and chopped

2 garlic cloves, minced

4 cups vegetable broth

2 tbsp extra virgin olive oil

1 tsp salt

black pepper, to serve

1 tbsp fresh thyme leaves, to serve

1 cup croûtons, to serve

Directions:

In a skillet, cook bacon until crisp. Drain on paper towels; set aside. Coarsely chop bacon and place in a microwave-safe pie plate.

Drizzle bacon with honey; cover with plastic wrap. Just before serving, cook in the microwave for 30 seconds.

Heat olive oil in a large pot and gently sauté the onion, celery and garlic until fragrant. Stir in vegetable broth, parsnips and salt, and bring to the boil.

Reduce heat and simmer for 30 minutes. Set aside to cool and blend until smooth. Garnish with croûtons, fresh thyme and chopped bacon.

Celery and Apple Soup

Serves: 4-5

Prep time: 20 min

Ingredients:

2 celery stalks, chopped

1 large apple, chopped

1/2 onion, chopped

2 carrots, chopped

1 garlic clove, minced

4 cups vegetable broth

3-4 tbsp extra virgin olive oil

1 tsp paprika

1 tsp grated ginger

salt and black pepper, to taste

Directions:

Heat olive oil in a deep soup pot over medium-high heat. Gently sauté onion, garlic and carrots for 3-4 minutes, stirring. Add in paprika, ginger, celery, apple and broth.

Bring to the boil then reduce heat and simmer, covered, for 10 minutes. Blend soup until smooth and return to pan. Cook over medium-high heat until heated through. Season with salt and pepper to taste and serve.

Sweet Potato and Coconut Soup

Serves: 4-5

Prep time: 35 min

Ingredients:

1 small onion, chopped

2 lb sweet potatoes, peeled and diced

4 cups vegetable broth

1 can coconut milk

2 tbsp extra virgin olive oil

1 tsp nutmeg

Directions:

Heat olive oil in a large saucepan over medium heat. Add onion and sauté until tender. Add in broth, sweet potato and nutmeg.

Bring to a boil then reduce heat and simmer, covered, for 30 minutes. Blend soup until smooth and cook for 2-3 minutes until heated through.

Broccoli and Zucchini Soup

Serves 6

Prep time: 35 min

Ingredients:

2 leeks, white part only, finely chopped

1 broccoli head, broken into florets

2 zucchinis, peeled and chopped

3 cups vegetable broth

1 cup water

3 tbsp extra virgin olive oil

4 oz blue cheese, crumbled

1/2 cup light cream

salt and black pepper, to taste

Directions:

Heat the olive oil in a large saucepan over medium heat. Gently sauté the leeks, stirring, for 5 minutes or until soft.

Add in broccoli, zucchinis, water and broth and bring to a boil. Reduce heat to low and simmer, stirring occasionally, for 20 minutes, or until vegetables are just tender. Remove from heat and set aside for 5 minutes to cool.

Transfer soup to a blender. Add in the cheese and blend in batches until smooth. Return to saucepan and place over low heat. Add in cream and stir to combine. Season with salt and pepper to taste.

Mediterranean Potato Soup

Serves 4-5

Prep time: 35 min

Ingredients:

4 red potatoes, diced

1 garlic clove, crushed

2 carrots, sliced

1 15-oz can red kidney beans, drained and rinsed

2 oz whole wheat noodles, uncooked

3 cups vegetable broth

3 tbsp extra virgin olive oil

2 cups fresh spinach

½ tsp dried rosemary

salt, to taste

black pepper, to taste

¼ cup grated Parmesan cheese

Directions:

Heat the olive oil over medium heat and sauté the onion, garlic, carrots and potatoes for 2-3 minutes. Add vegetable broth and rosemary and bring the soup to a boil.

Simmer 15 minutes then add kidney beans and noodles. Bring to boil again, cook until noodles are soft. Remove from heat, add spinach to pot and stir.

Ladle into bowls and serve with Parmesan cheese.

Spinach and Nettle Soup

Serves 4-5

Prep time: 35 min

Ingredients:

14 oz frozen spinach

1 lb young top shoots of nettles, well washed

1 large onion, chopped

1 carrot, chopped

4 cups water

3-4 tbsp extra virgin olive oil

1/4 cup white rice

1-2 cloves garlic, crushed

black pepper and salt, to taste

yogurt, to serve

Directions:

Clean the young nettles, wash and cook them in slightly salted water for 3-4 minutes. Drain, rinse, drain again and then chop or pass through a sieve.

Heat the oil in a cooking pot, add the onion and carrot and sauté together for a few minutes, until just softened. Add garlic and rice and stir.

Remove from heat. Add the spinach, nettles and about 2 cups of hot water. Season with salt and pepper, bring back to a boil, then reduce the heat and simmer for around 30 minutes.

Serve with yogurt.

Spinach Soup with Feta

Serves 4

Prep time: 35 min

Ingredients:

14 oz frozen spinach

5.5 oz feta cheese, crumbled

1 large onion, finely cut

2-3 tbsp light cream

3-4 tbsp extra virgin olive oil

1-2 garlic cloves, crushed

4 cups hot water

black pepper and salt, to taste

Directions:

Heat the oil in a cooking pot and sauté the onion and spinach and together for a few minutes, until just softened. Add in garlic and stir for a minute.

Remove from heat. Add water and season with salt and pepper. Bring back to the boil, then reduce heat and simmer for around 30 minutes.

Blend soup in a blender. Stir in the crumbled feta cheese and the cream. Serve hot.

FREE BONUS RECIPES: 20 Superfood Paleo and Vegan Smoothies for Vibrant Health and Easy Weight Loss

Kale and Kiwi Smoothie

Serves: 2

Prep time: 2-3 min

Ingredients:

2-3 ice cubes

1 cup orange juice

1 small pear, peeled and chopped

2 kiwi, peeled and chopped

2-3 kale leaves

2-3 dates, pitted

Directions:

Combine all ingredients in a high speed blender and blend until smooth.

Delicious Broccoli Smoothie

Serves: 2

Prep time: 2-3 min

Ingredients:

2-3 frozen broccoli florets

1 cup coconut milk

1 banana, peeled and chopped

1 cup pineapple, cut

1 peach, chopped

1 tsp cinnamon

Directions:

Combine all ingredients in a high speed blender and blend until smooth.

Papaya Smoothie

Serves: 2

Prep time: 2-3 min

Ingredients:

2-3 frozen broccoli florets

1 cup orange juice

1 small ripe avocado, peeled, cored and diced

1 cup papaya

1 cup fresh strawberries

Directions:

Combine all ingredients in a high speed blender and blend until smooth.

Beet and Papaya Smoothie

Serves: 2

Prep time: 2-3 min

Ingredients:

3-4 ice cubes

1 cup orange juice

1 banana, peeled and chopped

1 cup papaya

1 small beet, peeled and cut

Directions:

Combine all ingredients in a high speed blender and blend until smooth.

Lean Green Smoothie

Serves: 2

Prep time: 2-3 min

Ingredients:

1 frozen banana, chopped

1 cup orange juice

2-3 kale leaves, stems removed

1 small cucumber, peeled and chopped

1/2 cup fresh parsley leaves

½ tsp grated ginger

Directions:

Combine all ingredients in a high speed blender and blend until smooth.

Easy Antioxidant Smoothie

Serves: 2

Prep time: 2-3 min

Ingredients:

2-3 frozen broccoli florets

1 cup orange juice

2 plums, cut

1 cup raspberries

1 tsp ginger powder

Directions:

Combine all ingredients in a high speed blender and blend until smooth.

Healthy Purple Smoothie

Serves: 2

Prep time: 2-3 min

Ingredients:

2-3 frozen broccoli florets

1 cup water

1/2 avocado, peeled and chopped

3 plums, chopped

1 cup blueberries

Directions:

Combine all ingredients in a high speed blender and blend until smooth.

Mom's Favorite Kale Smoothie

Serves: 2

Prep time: 2-3 min

Ingredients:

2-3 ice cubes

1½ cup orange juice

1 green small apple, cut

½ cucumber, chopped

2-3 leaves kale

½ cup raspberries

Directions:

Combine all ingredients in a high speed blender and blend until smooth.

Creamy Green Smoothie

Serves: 2

Prep time: 2-3 min

Ingredients:

1 frozen banana

1 cup coconut milk

1 small pear, chopped

1 cup baby spinach

1 cup grapes

1 tbsp coconut butter

1 tsp vanilla extract

Directions:

Combine all ingredients in a high speed blender and blend until smooth.

Strawberry and Arugula Smoothie

Serves: 2

Prep time: 2-3 min

Ingredients:

2 cups frozen strawberries

1 cup unsweetened almond milk

10-12 arugula leaves

1/2 tsp ground cinnamon

Directions:

Combine ice, almond milk, strawberries, arugula and cinnamon in a high speed blender. Blend until smooth and serve.

Emma's Amazing Smoothie

Serves: 2

Prep time: 2-3 min

Ingredients:

1 frozen banana, chopped

1 cup orange juice

1 large nectarine, sliced

1/2 zucchini, peeled and chopped

2-3 dates, pitted

Directions:

Combine all ingredients in a high speed blender and blend until smooth.

Good-To-Go Morning Smoothie

Serves: 2

Prep time: 2-3 min

Ingredients:

1 cup frozen strawberries

1 cup apple juice

1 banana, chopped

1 cup raw asparagus, chopped

1 tbsp ground flaxseed

Directions:

Combine all ingredients in a high speed blender and blend until smooth.

Endless Energy Smoothie

Serves: 2

Prep time: 2-3 min

Ingredients:

1 frozen banana, chopped

11/2 cup green tea

1 cup chopped pineapple

2 raw asparagus spears, chopped

1 lime, juiced

1 tbsp chia seeds

Directions:

Combine all ingredients in a high speed blender and blend until smooth.

High-fibre Fruit Smoothie

Serves: 2

Prep time: 2-3 min

Ingredients:

1 frozen banana, chopped

1 cup orange juice

2 cups chopped papaya

1 cup shredded cabbage

1 tbsp chia seeds

Directions:

Combine all ingredients in a high speed blender and blend until smooth.

Nutritious Green Smoothie

Serves: 2

Prep time: 2-3 min

Ingredients:

2-3 frozen broccoli florets

1 cup apple juice

1 large pear, chopped

1 kiwi, peeled and chopped

1 cup spinach leaves

1-2 dates, pitted

Directions:

Combine all ingredients in a high speed blender and blend until smooth.

Apricot, Strawberry and Banana Smoothie

Serves: 2

Prep time: 2-3 min

Ingredients:

1 frozen banana

11/2 cup almond milk

5 dried apricots

1 cup fresh strawberries

Directions:

Combine all ingredients in a high speed blender and blend until smooth.

Spinach and Green Apple Smoothie

Serves: 2

Prep time: 2-3 min

Ingredients:

3-4 ice cubes

1 cup unsweetened almond milk

1 banana, peeled and chopped

2 green apples, peeled and chopped

1 cup raw spinach leaves

3-4 dates, pitted

1 tsp grated ginger

Directions:

Combine all ingredients in a high speed blender and blend until smooth.

Superfood Blueberry Smoothie

Serves: 2

Prep time: 2-3 min

Ingredients:

2-3 cubes frozen spinach

1 cup green tea

1 banana

2 cups blueberries

1 tbsp ground flaxseed

Directions:

Combine all ingredients in a high speed blender and blend until smooth.

Zucchini and Blueberry Smoothie

Serves: 2

Prep time: 2-3 min

Ingredients:

1 cup frozen blueberries

1 cup unsweetened almond milk

1 banana

1 zucchini, peeled and chopped

Directions:

Combine all ingredients in a high speed blender and blend until smooth.

Tropical Spinach Smoothie

Serves: 2

Prep time: 2-3 min

Ingredients:

1/2 cup crushed ice or 3-4 ice cubes

1 cup coconut milk

1 mango, peeled and diced

1 cup fresh spinach leaves

4-5 dates, pitted

1/2 tsp vanilla extract

Directions:

Combine all ingredients in a high speed blender and blend until smooth.

About the Author

Alissa Grey is a fitness and nutrition enthusiast who loves to teach people about losing weight and feeling better about themselves. She lives in a small French village in the foothills of a beautiful mountain range with her husband, three teenage kids, two free spirited dogs, and various other animals.

Alissa is incredibly lucky to be able to cook and eat natural foods, mostly grown nearby, something she's done since she was a teenager. She enjoys yoga, running, reading, hanging out with her family, and growing organic vegetables and herbs.

Made in the USA
Middletown, DE
11 November 2018